Grandma's Kitchen Chronicles

Recipes and Stories Passed Down Through Generations

CHRIS N. ETHAN

All rights reserved.No part of this publication may be reproduced, distributed, or transmitted in any form or by any means, including photocopying, recording, or other electronic or mechanical methods, without the prior written permission of the publisher, except in the case of brief quotations embodied in critical reviews and certain other noncommercial uses permitted by copyright law.

Copyright © MIKE VANOVER 2025

TABLE OF CONTENT

Chapter 1: A Legacy of Love – Grandma's Story

Chapter 2: The Comfort of Breakfast – Early Morning Delights

Chapter 3: Soups and Stews – Hearty Meals for Every Season

Chapter 4: The Art of Baking – Sweets from the Heart

Chapter 5: Sunday Dinners – The Feast That Brings Us Home

Chapter 6: Comforting Sides – Recipes That Complete the Meal

Chapter 7: Preserving the Harvest – Canning and Jams

Chapter 8: Around the Table – Special Occasions and Holiday Feasts

Chapter 9: Simple Pleasures – Everyday Comfort Foods

Chapter 10: The Passing of a Legacy – Keeping Grandma's Spirit Alive

Chapter 11: Conclusion – A Legacy of Flavor, Love, and Memories

Introduction

The Heart of Grandma's Kitchen

Food is more than just sustenance; it is an expression of love, tradition, and the stories we carry with us from one generation to the next. For many of us, the heart of our family's legacy can be found not in dusty heirlooms or ancient photographs, but in the recipes passed down through the years, often told around the family table. In *Grandma's Kitchen Chronicles: Recipes and Stories Passed Down Through Generations*, we celebrate the flavors, memories, and wisdom that come from Grandma's kitchen a space where time slows down and each meal tells a story.

From the moment you step into Grandma's kitchen, it's not just about the food; it's about the feeling that surrounds it. The soft hum of the stove, the rhythm of a spoon stirring a pot, the smell of fresh bread filling the air these are the memories that stay with us long after the meal is over. Grandma's kitchen is where we learned to chop, stir, bake, and share, where the passing of knowledge came not through instruction, but through the love and care embedded in every meal.

For generations, families have come together in kitchens to bond over food, pass down traditions, and share the knowledge that makes a recipe truly special. These recipes are often more than just a collection of ingredients they are a testament to a time when meals were made with patience, a touch of creativity, and a deep understanding of the importance of family. They are full of little secrets, tips, and tricks that turn a simple dish into a masterpiece.

In this cookbook, we've gathered some of the best-loved recipes from Grandma's kitchen, each one a reflection of the love, labor, and life that went into it. Whether it's the Sunday roast that brought the family together, the sweet desserts that marked special occasions, or the hearty stews that warmed our hearts on cold days, each recipe carries with it a piece of history.

But beyond the recipes, *Grandma's Kitchen Chronicles* is about the stories that make them special. Each dish has a history, a meaning, and a memory attached to it the story of how it came to be, who first made it, and why it has become a cherished part of the family's tradition. For every recipe in this book, there is a story of laughter in the kitchen, of messes made and cleaned, of patience learned, and of love shared.

This cookbook is more than a collection of recipes; it is a way to carry Grandma's spirit forward. It is a way to teach the next generation the importance of good food, the value of tradition, and the art of making a meal with love. Through these pages, we hope to inspire you to create your own memories in the kitchen, to pass on these recipes to your children and grandchildren, and to always remember that the best meals are the ones made with heart.

As you turn the pages of this cookbook, you'll find not only the meals that have fed our family through the years but also the stories that have fed our souls. From Grandma's signature pie that she made every holiday, to the simple soup that healed us when we were sick, each recipe represents a memory a moment in time that continues to live on with every new generation.

So, gather your loved ones around, roll up your sleeves, and let the heart of Grandma's kitchen guide you. These recipes are more than just instructions; they are a reminder that food is not just something we eat, but something we share, something we create together, and something that binds us to the people we love and the memories we hold dear.

Chapter 1: A Legacy of Love – Grandma's Story

Grandma wasn't just the matriarch of the family; she was the heart of it. For as long as I can remember, her kitchen was always a place of warmth, a haven where the world outside could fade away, and only the rhythm of chopping vegetables, stirring pots, and laughter filled the air. Every meal she prepared was a masterpiece, not just in taste but in the stories it carried stories of the past, of struggles, of triumphs, and of love.

Grandma's culinary journey didn't start in the modern, well-equipped kitchens we have today. Her kitchen was a modest space, one that grew from the simplest of beginnings into the soul of our family. It was there, with the smell of freshly baked bread wafting through the house, that we all gathered, shared stories, and learned lessons that would stay with us forever. But for Grandma, cooking was never just about making food it was about nurturing the spirit, about providing not just nourishment but comfort, and a sense of belonging.

Born into a family where resources were scarce but love was abundant, Grandma's early years were spent learning the art of cooking from her mother, who came from a long line of women who had mastered the kitchen. With every recipe passed down through the generations, she learned the importance of using what you had, making the most of every ingredient, and, most importantly, the value of patience in cooking. For Grandma, cooking wasn't rushed; it was about taking time to let the flavors develop, about understanding the magic that could happen when you gave love to your food.

She often told us stories about her childhood, how she had to get creative with the ingredients they had available during tough times. With limited access to fresh produce and meats, Grandma became a master of simple, hearty meals that could feed a family on a tight budget. She had a knack for turning the most basic ingredients like beans, potatoes, and grains into something magical. It wasn't the quality of the ingredients that made the food great, but the care and attention she gave to each dish.

One of her fondest stories was about her first attempt at making a pie. She had just gotten married and, eager to impress her new husband, decided to make a cherry pie from scratch. Without the luxury of pre-made crusts or canned fillings, she used what she had: flour, butter, sugar, and fresh cherries from the tree outside. It was her first time baking a pie, and while the crust didn't turn out as perfectly as she hoped, it tasted like love sweet, imperfect, but unforgettable. Her husband raved about it, and that memory stayed with her for the rest of her life. That pie was her first lesson in the importance of trying, of learning from mistakes, and of knowing that love could make even the simplest of dishes extraordinary.

As the years went by, Grandma's kitchen became the gathering place for our entire family. Every Sunday, without fail, the house would be filled with the aroma of roast chicken, mashed potatoes, and her famous stuffing. We would all sit around the table, sharing not just the meal, but the stories of our lives our triumphs, our troubles, our joys, and our heartaches. Grandma had a way of making each of us feel heard and valued, and her food was always the anchor that held us together.

She never wrote down her recipes. They were in her head, passed down through years of practice and intuition. But for us, the family, her recipes were more than just instructions they were a roadmap of who she was, a reflection of the love, strength, and creativity she poured into every meal. Each recipe told a story, each ingredient was a piece of history, and each dish was an expression of the love she had for her family.

As time went on, Grandma's health began to decline, but her love for cooking never wavered. Even in her later years, she would still find a way to make her signature dishes, often with a little help from us. It was during these times that we realized how deeply cooking had become a part of her identity. It wasn't just about the food; it was about the act of nurturing, the act of giving. Even when she could no longer stand in the kitchen for hours, her hands were still able to prepare the same dishes we had grown up with. It was as though her spirit lingered in every pot, in every simmering soup, and in every warm loaf of bread.

Her legacy is not just in the recipes she left behind but in the love she infused into every meal, in the lessons she taught us without ever saying a word. Grandma's kitchen was where we learned to appreciate the beauty of simple, honest cooking. She taught us that food is not just fuel, but a way to connect with each other, to show love, to nurture, and to create lasting memories.

In this chapter, I want to share with you some of the recipes that Grandma passed down through the years the ones that have become staples in our family, the ones that continue to bring us together, even after she's gone. These recipes are more than just food; they are her spirit, her love, and her wisdom, wrapped in every bite.

Recipes Passed Down Through Generations:

- Grandma's Homemade Bread
  A simple, yet beloved recipe that Grandma made almost every week. It's warm, comforting, and always brings the family together. She would bake it fresh for every Sunday dinner, filling the

house with the delicious smell of rising dough.

- **Grandpa's Favorite Honey Butter**
  A sweet and creamy spread made with butter, honey, and a touch of cinnamon, this recipe was a family favorite. It would be spread generously on fresh bread, pancakes, and waffles, and sometimes even enjoyed by the spoonful!

Through these pages, I want to pass on Grandma's legacy her wisdom, her love for cooking, and her ability to create meals that made us feel at home. Each recipe holds a piece of her heart, and now, it's time to share that with you.

This chapter sets the tone for the rest of the book, creating a deep emotional connection with the reader and introducing the significance of the recipes that will follow. Let me know if you'd like to adjust or expand on any part!

Chapter 2: The Comfort of Breakfast – Early Morning Delights

There's something magical about breakfast in Grandma's kitchen. The moment the sun began to rise, the smell of freshly brewed coffee, sizzling bacon, and warm pancakes would fill the air, pulling us out of bed and towards the heart of the house. Breakfast wasn't just a meal; it was an experience. It was the first time we gathered together in the morning, the time when we could talk, laugh, and share plans for the day. It was the beginning of each new day, and Grandma made sure that every breakfast was full of love, warmth, and flavor.

One of my favorite memories is waking up to the sound of Grandma humming as she flipped pancakes in the kitchen. Her pancakes were legendary golden brown on the outside, fluffy on the inside, and perfectly paired with syrup and butter. But what made them so special wasn't just the taste; it was the ritual. Grandma would always serve the pancakes with fresh fruit, a dollop of whipped cream, and a side of crispy bacon. She would ask us how we slept, how our dreams had been, and if there was anything exciting planned for the day. In those quiet morning moments, you could feel the love and care that went into every plate.

Breakfast with Grandma was more than just the food; it was about creating memories. It was about being present in the moment, sitting at the kitchen table, and savoring the first meal of the day together. Each dish had a purpose to nourish not just our bodies but our souls. And for Grandma, it was never rushed. No matter how busy the day ahead seemed, breakfast was always something special.

In this chapter, I want to share some of the most cherished breakfast recipes that have been passed down through our family. These recipes are more than just food; they are a reflection of the love, care, and connection we shared every morning around Grandma's table. Whether you're making pancakes on a lazy Saturday morning or preparing a special breakfast for your loved ones, these recipes will bring you the warmth and comfort of home.

Recipes for Early Morning Delights:

- **Grandma's Buttermilk Pancakes**
  Grandma's pancakes were soft, fluffy, and light the kind you could pile high and drench with maple syrup or fresh berries. The buttermilk gave them a tangy flavor that balanced perfectly with the sweetness of the syrup. They were

always served with crispy bacon, scrambled eggs, and sometimes a drizzle of homemade strawberry jam.

Ingredients:

- 2 cups all-purpose flour
- 2 tablespoons sugar
- 2 teaspoons baking powder
- 1/2 teaspoon baking soda
- 1/4 teaspoon salt
- 2 large eggs
- 2 cups buttermilk
- 1/4 cup melted butter
- 1 teaspoon vanilla extract

- Instructions:

  - In a large bowl, whisk together flour, sugar, baking powder, baking soda, and salt.

- In a separate bowl, whisk the eggs, then add the buttermilk, melted butter, and vanilla extract.

- Pour the wet ingredients into the dry ingredients and stir gently until just combined (be careful not to overmix).

- Heat a griddle or non-stick pan over medium heat and lightly grease with butter.

- Pour 1/4 cup of batter onto the griddle and cook until bubbles form on the surface, then flip and cook until golden brown.

- Serve with your favorite toppings — syrup, butter, fresh fruit, or whipped cream.

- **Cinnamon-Sugar Biscuits**

  These biscuits were a breakfast staple in Grandma's house. Soft and buttery on the inside, with a crisp, sweet crust on the outside, they were always the perfect addition to a morning spread. Grandma would often serve them warm, right out of the oven, with a pat of butter or a spoonful of honey.

Ingredients:

- 2 cups all-purpose flour
- 2 teaspoons baking powder
- 1/4 teaspoon baking soda
- 1/2 teaspoon salt
- 1/4 cup cold butter
- 3/4 cup buttermilk
- 1/2 cup sugar
- 1 teaspoon ground cinnamon

- Instructions:

  - Preheat the oven to 425°F (220°C).
  - In a large bowl, mix the flour, baking powder, baking soda, and salt.
  - Cut in the butter until the mixture resembles coarse crumbs.
  - Add the buttermilk and stir just until the dough comes together.

- Turn the dough out onto a floured surface and gently knead until smooth.
- Roll the dough to about 1/2-inch thickness and cut into rounds.
- Place biscuits on a greased baking sheet and bake for 12-15 minutes or until golden.
- Mix sugar and cinnamon together and sprinkle over the biscuits as soon as they come out of the oven.

- **Eggs in a Basket: A Breakfast with a Story**
  This dish was one of Grandma's most creative ways to cook eggs. It was simple yet elegant, and the family always loved it. The story goes that she first made this dish for a special breakfast one morning when she couldn't find a frying pan. She used a round cookie cutter to cut out the center of a slice of bread and cooked the egg inside. It became an instant favorite.

  Ingredients:
  - 2 slices of bread
  - 2 eggs

- 1 tablespoon butter
- Salt and pepper to taste

- **Instructions:**
  - Use a round cookie cutter or a glass to cut a hole in the center of each slice of bread.
  - Heat the butter in a frying pan over medium heat.
  - Place the slices of bread in the pan and crack an egg into the hole in each slice.
  - Cook until the egg whites are set and the yolk is cooked to your liking. Season with salt and pepper.
  - Serve with a side of crispy bacon or fresh fruit.

- **Blueberry Muffins**
  Soft, moist, and bursting with fresh blueberries, these muffins were a favorite for breakfast, especially when Grandma had a fresh batch of blueberries from the garden. She would bake them in the early morning and serve them still warm with a dollop of butter.

Ingredients:

- 2 cups all-purpose flour
- 1 tablespoon baking powder
- 1/2 teaspoon salt
- 1/2 cup sugar
- 1/2 cup milk
- 1/4 cup vegetable oil
- 2 large eggs
- 1 teaspoon vanilla extract
- 1 cup fresh blueberries

- **Instructions:**

  - Preheat the oven to 375°F (190°C).
  - In a bowl, mix together the flour, baking powder, salt, and sugar.
  - In another bowl, whisk the milk, vegetable oil, eggs, and vanilla extract.

- Combine the wet ingredients with the dry ingredients, stirring just until combined.
- Gently fold in the blueberries.
- Spoon the batter into a greased muffin tin and bake for 20-25 minutes, or until golden.

- **Crispy Bacon and Homemade Hash Browns**
  No breakfast was complete without bacon and crispy hash browns. The bacon, always perfectly crisp and golden, was cooked slowly to preserve its flavor, while the hash browns were crunchy on the outside and soft on the inside. This combination became a signature feature of breakfast at Grandma's house.

  Ingredients:
  - 4 slices of bacon
  - 2 large potatoes, peeled and grated
  - 1 tablespoon vegetable oil
  - Salt and pepper to taste

- Instructions:

- For the bacon: Cook the bacon in a skillet over medium heat until crisp. Remove from the pan and drain on paper towels.

- For the hash browns: Squeeze excess moisture from the grated potatoes using a clean kitchen towel.

- Heat the oil in a skillet over medium heat. Add the grated potatoes, pressing them down into a flat layer.

- Cook for 4-5 minutes on each side until crispy and golden. Season with salt and pepper.

This chapter, filled with comfort food classics, offers a window into the early morning routines of a family gathered around the table for a breakfast that was as much about the love and togetherness as it was about the food itself. Let me know if you'd like me to proceed with the next chapter or adjust anything!

Chapter 3: Soups and Stews – Hearty Meals for Every Season

There's something undeniably comforting about a bowl of soup or stew. It's a meal that warms you from the inside out, filling you not only with nourishment but with a deep sense of satisfaction and contentment. In Grandma's kitchen, soups and stews were not just recipes; they were a reflection of her love for her family. Each pot simmered for hours, letting the flavors meld together in a way that made every bite feel like a hug.

I can still recall the sight of Grandma standing over the stove, stirring a large pot of soup, her face focused but serene. She would always make enough to feed the whole family, with plenty of leftovers for the next day or for someone who was feeling under the weather. Soup was her remedy for everything: a cold, a broken heart, or just a long, tiring day. It was her way of saying, "I'm here, and I've got you."

Grandma had an intuitive understanding of what made a great soup. She knew that the key wasn't always in the ingredients but in the time you allowed them to come together. The broth had to be just right, the vegetables tender but not mushy, and the seasoning balanced perfectly. It wasn't just about following a recipe it was about knowing when it was time to stir, when to add a little more salt, and when to let the soup sit for just a little longer so the flavors could deepen.

In this chapter, I'll share some of Grandma's favorite soup and stew recipes the ones that were always there for us, no matter the season. Whether you're making a pot of hearty stew for a cold winter evening or preparing a light, fresh soup for a spring afternoon, these recipes will remind you of the love and care that goes into every bowl.

Recipes for Hearty Soups and Stews:

- **Grandma's Chicken Soup**
  This was the ultimate comfort food. It was the first thing we would make if someone was feeling sick, and it was always served with a side of love and care. The combination of tender chicken, fresh vegetables, and savory broth made this soup a family favorite for generations.

  Ingredients:

    - 1 whole chicken, cut into pieces
    - 2 carrots, peeled and sliced

- 2 celery stalks, chopped
- 1 onion, chopped
- 4 garlic cloves, minced
- 8 cups chicken broth
- 1 teaspoon dried thyme
- 1 bay leaf
- Salt and pepper to taste
- 1 cup egg noodles or rice (optional)
- Fresh parsley for garnish

- **Instructions:**
  - In a large pot, combine the chicken, carrots, celery, onion, garlic, and chicken broth.
  - Bring the mixture to a boil, then reduce the heat and simmer for 45 minutes to 1 hour, until the chicken is fully cooked and tender.
  - Remove the chicken from the pot and shred the meat, discarding the bones.

Return the chicken to the pot.

- Add thyme, bay leaf, salt, and pepper. If you're adding noodles or rice, add them now and cook until tender.

- Remove the bay leaf and serve the soup hot, garnished with fresh parsley.

- **Beef Stew with Root Vegetables**
  Hearty and filling, this beef stew was always a crowd-pleaser. The tender chunks of beef, simmered with carrots, potatoes, and parsnips, created a comforting dish that could stand alone as a meal. Grandma made this stew when the weather turned colder, and it always paired perfectly with a slice of fresh bread.

  Ingredients:

  - 2 lbs beef stew meat, cut into chunks
  - 4 carrots, peeled and sliced
  - 4 potatoes, peeled and cubed
  - 2 parsnips, peeled and sliced
  - 1 onion, chopped

- 4 garlic cloves, minced
- 4 cups beef broth
- 2 tablespoons tomato paste
- 1 teaspoon dried thyme
- 1 bay leaf
- Salt and pepper to taste
- 2 tablespoons flour (optional, for thickening)

- **Instructions:**
  - In a large pot, brown the beef stew meat in a bit of oil over medium-high heat. Remove the beef and set it aside.
  - In the same pot, sauté the onion and garlic until softened.
  - Add the beef back into the pot along with the carrots, potatoes, parsnips, beef broth, tomato paste, thyme, bay leaf, salt, and pepper.
  - Bring to a boil, then reduce the heat and simmer for 1.5 to 2 hours, until the beef is

tender and the vegetables are cooked through.

- If you want a thicker stew, mix 2 tablespoons of flour with a little water to make a slurry, and stir it into the stew. Simmer for another 10 minutes to thicken.

- Serve hot with crusty bread.

- **Vegetable Barley Soup: The Healer**
  This was a favorite in Grandma's house, especially when the weather was changing. Packed with fiber and nutrients from the vegetables and barley, this soup was as healthy as it was delicious. It was perfect for both cold days and as a light meal when you needed a bit of comfort without feeling too heavy.

  Ingredients:

  - 1 cup pearl barley, rinsed

  - 4 cups vegetable broth

  - 2 carrots, peeled and diced

  - 2 celery stalks, chopped

- 1 onion, chopped
- 2 garlic cloves, minced
- 1 zucchini, diced
- 1 cup spinach, chopped
- 1 teaspoon dried basil
- 1 teaspoon dried oregano
- Salt and pepper to taste
- 1 tablespoon olive oil

- **Instructions:**
  - Heat olive oil in a large pot over medium heat. Add the onion, garlic, carrots, and celery, and sauté for about 5 minutes until softened.
  - Add the vegetable broth, barley, zucchini, basil, oregano, salt, and pepper. Bring to a boil.
  - Reduce the heat to low and simmer for 45 minutes to 1 hour, until the barley is tender.

- Add the spinach and cook for another 5 minutes, until wilted.

- Serve hot, and garnish with fresh herbs or a sprinkle of Parmesan cheese if desired.

- **Split Pea Soup with Ham**

    This hearty, satisfying soup was a family favorite for its rich flavor and comforting texture. The combination of split peas and smoky ham created a dish that was perfect for warming up after a long day. Grandma always made this when she had leftover ham from a holiday meal, turning it into a delicious, filling soup that everyone loved.

    Ingredients:

    - 2 cups dried split peas, rinsed
    - 1 lb ham bone or ham hock
    - 4 cups chicken broth
    - 2 carrots, peeled and chopped
    - 2 celery stalks, chopped
    - 1 onion, chopped

- 2 garlic cloves, minced
- 1 bay leaf
- Salt and pepper to taste

- **Instructions:**
  - In a large pot, combine the split peas, ham bone, chicken broth, carrots, celery, onion, garlic, and bay leaf.
  - Bring to a boil, then reduce the heat and simmer for 1.5 to 2 hours, until the peas are soft and the soup has thickened.
  - Remove the ham bone, shred the meat, and return it to the pot.
  - Season with salt and pepper to taste, and serve hot.

This chapter highlights the warmth and comfort that soups and stews can bring to any table. The slow simmering, the deep flavors, and the way these dishes are meant to be shared with loved ones are central to the legacy Grandma left behind. Whether served on a chilly winter night or a busy weekday evening, these dishes will nourish both body and soul.

Let me know if you'd like to proceed with the next chapter!

Chapter 4: The Art of Baking – Sweets from the Heart

Baking was never just a task in Grandma's kitchen; it was an act of love. From the scent of cookies wafting through the house to the joy of watching her pull a perfectly golden pie from the oven, baking was her way of bringing warmth and comfort to every occasion. It didn't matter if it was a special holiday, a birthday, or just a regular afternoon when Grandma baked, it felt like the world was a little bit sweeter.

For Grandma, baking was an art form. She had an intuitive understanding of how ingredients worked together to create magic. She never measured with precision; instead, she'd rely on her senses the smell of vanilla, the feel of the dough, the sound of a crust crisping in the oven. She knew that baking wasn't just about following recipes; it was about understanding the rhythm of the ingredients and the warmth of the oven.

I remember standing by Grandma's side, watching her carefully mix flour, sugar, and butter together to create the dough for her famous cookies. She would always let us help, teaching us how to knead, roll, and cut out perfect shapes. Her kitchen was a safe haven where we learned not just how to bake, but how to appreciate the simple joy of creating something beautiful with our hands.

Baking, to Grandma, wasn't just about making sweet treats. It was about creating memories, fostering connection, and showing love. A batch of cookies wasn't just a snack; it was a reminder that you were cared for. A freshly baked pie wasn't just dessert; it was Grandma's way of saying, "You're home."

In this chapter, I'm sharing some of Grandma's most beloved baking recipes. These aren't just sweets; they are expressions of love, tradition, and the simple joy of making something with your own two hands. Whether you're baking for a special occasion or just because, these recipes will fill your home with the same warmth and love that Grandma's kitchen always had.

Recipes for Sweets from the Heart:

- **Apple Pie with a Secret Ingredient**
  This was Grandma's signature pie, the one everyone looked forward to at Thanksgiving and family gatherings. What made it so special was the secret ingredient she added — a pinch of nutmeg and a dash of cinnamon to enhance the natural sweetness of the apples. The flaky crust, golden and buttery, was always a perfect balance with the juicy, spiced filling.

Ingredients:

- 6 cups sliced apples (Granny Smith or Honeycrisp work well)
- 1 tablespoon lemon juice
- 1/2 cup granulated sugar
- 1/4 cup packed brown sugar
- 1 tablespoon all-purpose flour
- 1 teaspoon ground cinnamon
- 1/4 teaspoon ground nutmeg
- 1/4 teaspoon salt
- 1 tablespoon butter
- 1 egg (for egg wash)
- 1 package pie crust (or homemade if preferred)

- Instructions:
  - Preheat your oven to 425°F (220°C).

- In a large bowl, toss the sliced apples with lemon juice.
- In a small bowl, combine the granulated sugar, brown sugar, flour, cinnamon, nutmeg, and salt.
- Add the sugar mixture to the apples and toss to coat evenly.
- Roll out the bottom pie crust and place it in a pie dish. Fill the crust with the apple mixture and dot with butter.
- Roll out the top crust, place it over the apples, and trim the edges. Crimp the edges together and cut a few slits in the top to allow steam to escape.
- Brush the top crust with a beaten egg to give it a golden color.
- Bake for 45-50 minutes, until the crust is golden brown and the filling is bubbling.
- Let it cool before serving.

- **Chocolate Chip Cookies That Melt in Your Mouth**

  Grandma's chocolate chip cookies were always a crowd favorite. They were soft in the middle, slightly crisp on the edges, and packed with gooey, melted chocolate. Her secret was in the butter-to-sugar ratio, which made the cookies perfectly chewy and rich.

Ingredients:

- 2 1/4 cups all-purpose flour
- 1/2 teaspoon baking soda
- 1 cup unsalted butter, softened
- 3/4 cup granulated sugar
- 3/4 cup packed brown sugar
- 1 teaspoon vanilla extract
- 2 large eggs
- 2 cups semisweet chocolate chips
- 1/2 teaspoon salt

- **Instructions:**
  - Preheat the oven to 350°F (175°C).

- In a bowl, whisk together the flour, baking soda, and salt.
- In another bowl, cream the butter, granulated sugar, and brown sugar until light and fluffy.
- Add the eggs, one at a time, followed by the vanilla extract. Mix until well combined.
- Gradually add the dry ingredients to the wet ingredients, mixing until combined.
- Stir in the chocolate chips.
- Drop tablespoon-sized scoops of dough onto a baking sheet lined with parchment paper.
- Bake for 9-11 minutes, or until the edges are golden but the centers are still soft.
- Cool on the baking sheet for a few minutes before transferring to a wire rack.

- **Grandma's Famous Cinnamon Rolls**
  These cinnamon rolls were the centerpiece of many Sunday mornings in Grandma's house. The dough was soft and buttery, the filling was cinnamon-sweet, and the cream cheese frosting

was the perfect finishing touch. Each roll was a little spiral of joy, and they were always gone before noon.

Ingredients for Dough:

- 1 cup warm milk
- 1/4 cup sugar
- 2 1/4 teaspoons active dry yeast
- 1/2 cup butter, softened
- 2 eggs
- 4 cups all-purpose flour
- 1/2 teaspoon salt

- **Ingredients for Filling:**
  - 1/2 cup butter, softened
  - 1 cup brown sugar
  - 2 tablespoons ground cinnamon
- **Ingredients for Frosting:**

- 1/2 cup cream cheese, softened
- 2 cups powdered sugar
- 2 tablespoons milk
- 1 teaspoon vanilla extract

- **Instructions:**
    - For the dough: In a bowl, combine warm milk, sugar, and yeast. Let sit for 5-10 minutes until frothy.
    - Add the butter, eggs, flour, and salt. Mix until a dough forms, then knead for 5-7 minutes until smooth and elastic.
    - Place the dough in a greased bowl, cover with a cloth, and let rise for 1-2 hours, or until doubled in size.
    - For the filling: Mix the softened butter, brown sugar, and cinnamon in a bowl.
    - Roll the dough into a rectangle and spread the filling evenly over the dough.
    - Roll up the dough tightly and cut into 12 even slices.

- Place the rolls in a greased baking pan and let rise for another hour.

- Preheat the oven to 375°F (190°C) and bake for 18-20 minutes, or until golden brown.

- For the frosting: Mix cream cheese, powdered sugar, milk, and vanilla extract until smooth. Spread over the warm rolls.

- Serve warm and enjoy the gooey goodness!

- **Pecan Pie with a Dash of Bourbon**
  Grandma's pecan pie was a holiday favorite, but honestly, we'd enjoy it any time of the year. The crust was buttery, the filling rich and gooey, with the crunch of toasted pecans. The addition of bourbon gave it a complex depth of flavor that made it unforgettable.

  Ingredients:

  - 1 pie crust (homemade or store-bought)
  - 1 1/2 cups pecan halves
  - 3/4 cup light corn syrup

- 1/4 cup brown sugar
- 1/4 cup melted butter
- 3 large eggs
- 2 tablespoons bourbon
- 1 teaspoon vanilla extract
- 1/4 teaspoon salt

- **Instructions:**
  - Preheat the oven to 350°F (175°C).
  - In a bowl, whisk together the corn syrup, brown sugar, melted butter, eggs, bourbon, vanilla extract, and salt.
  - Stir in the pecans and pour the mixture into the pie crust.
  - Bake for 45-50 minutes, or until the filling is set and slightly golden on top.
  - Let the pie cool completely before slicing. Serve with a dollop of whipped cream or vanilla ice cream.

Baking with Grandma was always about more than just following recipes. It was about learning to be patient, appreciating the beauty in simple ingredients, and sharing the joy of creating something from scratch. These recipes, passed down through generations, are a testament to the love and care Grandma put into everything she baked. Let these sweet treats fill your home with the same warmth and happiness that Grandma's kitchen always had.

Chapter 5: Sunday Dinners – The Feast That Brings Us Home

Sunday dinners were a time for the entire family to gather, reconnect, and enjoy the fruits of Grandma's labor. These meals weren't just about the food they were about family, tradition, and a sense of belonging. Every Sunday, without fail, the house would be filled with the smells of roast meats, fresh-baked bread, and the hearty side dishes that accompanied each feast. It was a time when we could all put aside our busy lives and focus on each other, sharing stories, laughter, and love over a meal that had been carefully prepared with great care and patience.

I remember how Grandma would start the preparations early in the morning. The roasting pan would be placed in the oven with a beautifully seasoned roast, and the house would begin to fill with the intoxicating scent of herbs and spices. Her kitchen was always organized every dish had its place, every ingredient had its purpose. As the day went on, she would set the table, pulling out the good china, polishing the silverware, and making sure everything was perfect. But it wasn't about perfection; it was about creating an atmosphere where we felt loved and cherished.

Sunday dinners were Grandma's way of saying, "You are important, and you matter." She poured not just ingredients into the meal but a part of herself. The table was always set with an array of dishes, each one holding a memory, a lesson, or a cherished tradition. Whether it was the roast chicken that she'd stuffed with herbs from her garden, the mashed potatoes that were always creamy and rich, or the green beans she'd sautéed with garlic and butter, each dish was a reflection of her love and dedication to her family.

It wasn't just about the main course, either. Sunday dinners also featured the special sides that we had all come to love from the buttery mashed potatoes to the sweet, candied carrots. And, of course, there was always room for dessert. No Sunday meal was complete without Grandma's famous apple pie or her velvety chocolate cake. These were the moments when we gathered together, broke bread, and created memories that would last a lifetime.

In this chapter, I want to share with you some of the most treasured recipes from Sunday dinners at Grandma's house. These dishes have been passed down through generations, and each one represents a time when the whole family came together, laughing, eating, and creating memories. Whether you're making a Sunday roast for your family or hosting a special occasion, these recipes will bring you a little closer to the warmth and love that Grandma's kitchen always provided.

Recipes for Sunday Dinners:

- **Roast Chicken with Herb Stuffing**

  Grandma's roast chicken was the centerpiece of every Sunday dinner. Seasoned simply with salt, pepper, and fresh herbs from her garden, the chicken was roasted until golden brown, crispy on the outside and tender on the inside. The stuffing, made with bread cubes, celery, onions, and fresh herbs, was the perfect complement to the rich, flavorful chicken.

  Ingredients for Chicken:

    - 1 whole chicken (4-5 pounds)
    - 1 tablespoon olive oil
    - 1 tablespoon butter
    - 2 teaspoons salt
    - 1 teaspoon pepper
    - 2 sprigs rosemary
    - 2 sprigs thyme

- 1 lemon, halved
- 1 onion, quartered

- **Ingredients for Stuffing:**
  - 6 cups bread cubes (preferably day-old bread)
  - 1/2 cup butter
  - 1 onion, chopped
  - 2 celery stalks, chopped
  - 2 teaspoons dried sage
  - 1 teaspoon dried thyme
  - 1 cup chicken broth
  - Salt and pepper to taste

- **Instructions for Chicken:**
  - Preheat the oven to 425°F (220°C).
  - Rub the chicken with olive oil, butter, salt, and pepper.

- Stuff the chicken with rosemary, thyme, lemon halves, and onion.
- Place the chicken on a roasting rack in a roasting pan and roast for 1.5 to 2 hours, or until the internal temperature reaches 165°F (74°C).
- Let the chicken rest before carving.

- **Instructions for Stuffing:**

    - In a large skillet, melt the butter over medium heat. Add the onion and celery and sauté until softened.
    - Add the sage, thyme, salt, and pepper, and stir to combine.
    - Add the bread cubes and toss to coat evenly with the butter mixture.
    - Gradually add the chicken broth until the stuffing is moistened but not soggy.
    - Stuff the chicken with the mixture or bake it separately in a greased baking dish for 30 minutes.

- **Mashed Potatoes with Grandma's Special Gravy**

These mashed potatoes were always creamy and rich, made with butter, cream, and just the right amount of seasoning. Grandma's gravy was always the perfect accompaniment — rich, savory, and smooth, made with the drippings from the roast chicken.

Ingredients for Mashed Potatoes:

- 4 pounds potatoes, peeled and cubed
- 1/2 cup unsalted butter
- 1 cup heavy cream
- Salt and pepper to taste
- Fresh parsley for garnish

- **Ingredients for Gravy:**
    - 1/4 cup chicken drippings or butter
    - 2 tablespoons all-purpose flour
    - 2 cups chicken broth
    - Salt and pepper to taste

- **Instructions for Mashed Potatoes:**

- Boil the potatoes in salted water until tender, about 15-20 minutes.
- Drain the potatoes and return them to the pot.
- Add the butter and heavy cream, then mash until smooth and creamy.
- Season with salt and pepper to taste, and garnish with fresh parsley.

- **Instructions for Gravy:**
    - In a small saucepan, melt the drippings or butter over medium heat.
    - Whisk in the flour and cook for 1-2 minutes, until golden.
    - Gradually add the chicken broth, whisking constantly to avoid lumps.
    - Simmer for 5-7 minutes, until the gravy thickens. Season with salt and pepper to taste.

- **Carrot Cake with Cream Cheese Frosting**
  For dessert, Grandma often made her famous carrot cake. It was perfectly spiced, moist, and rich with shredded carrots, walnuts, and a

velvety cream cheese frosting. Every slice was a little piece of heaven.

Ingredients for Carrot Cake:

- 2 cups all-purpose flour
- 1 1/2 teaspoons baking powder
- 1 teaspoon baking soda
- 1 1/2 teaspoons ground cinnamon
- 1/2 teaspoon ground nutmeg
- 1/2 teaspoon salt
- 1 1/2 cups granulated sugar
- 4 large eggs
- 1 cup vegetable oil
- 2 cups grated carrots
- 1/2 cup chopped walnuts

- **Ingredients for Cream Cheese Frosting:**
  - 8 oz cream cheese, softened

- 1/2 cup unsalted butter, softened
- 4 cups powdered sugar
- 1 teaspoon vanilla extract

- **Instructions for Cake:**
  - Preheat the oven to 350°F (175°C). Grease and flour two 9-inch cake pans.
  - In a bowl, combine the flour, baking powder, baking soda, cinnamon, nutmeg, and salt.
  - In another bowl, whisk together the sugar, eggs, and oil. Add the dry ingredients and mix until combined.
  - Stir in the grated carrots and walnuts.
  - Divide the batter between the two pans and bake for 30-35 minutes, or until a toothpick inserted into the center comes out clean.
  - Let the cakes cool completely before frosting.

- **Instructions for Frosting:**

- In a bowl, beat the cream cheese and butter together until smooth.

- Gradually add the powdered sugar and vanilla extract, and beat until fluffy.

- Frost the cooled cakes with the cream cheese frosting.

- **Green Bean Almondine**
  A simple, elegant side dish, green bean almondine was always a favorite at Sunday dinner. The green beans were blanched and then sautéed in butter, garlic, and toasted almonds, creating a dish that was both light and flavorful.

  Ingredients:

  - 1 pound fresh green beans, trimmed
  - 1/4 cup unsalted butter
  - 1/4 cup sliced almonds
  - 2 garlic cloves, minced
  - Salt and pepper to taste
  - Lemon wedges for garnish

- Instructions:

    - Bring a large pot of salted water to a boil. Add the green beans and cook for 3-4 minutes, until tender but still crisp.

    - Drain and set aside.

    - In a skillet, melt the butter over medium heat. Add the almonds and cook for 2-3 minutes, until golden.

    - Add the garlic and cook for another 30 seconds.

    - Add the cooked green beans and toss to coat in the butter and almonds. Season with salt and pepper, and serve with lemon wedges.

Sunday dinners at Grandma's house were more than just meals; they were gatherings that brought the family together, creating bonds that lasted long after the last bite. These recipes reflect that sense of connection, tradition, and the deep love that Grandma poured into every dish. Let these meals bring your family closer together, just as they did for us.

Chapter 6: Comforting Sides – Recipes That Complete the Meal

While the main course often stole the spotlight at Grandma's Sunday dinners, it was the side dishes that made the meal feel complete. These were the dishes that you looked forward to just as much as the roast chicken or the pot roast. Grandma had a gift for taking simple ingredients and turning them into something special something that complemented the main dish, but also stood proudly on its own.

Her sides were always made with love and care, whether it was the smooth mashed potatoes, the crisp green beans, or the buttery corn on the cob. Each one was created with the same attention to detail as the main dish, and each bite had its own story to tell.

Some of my fondest memories are of standing next to Grandma as she prepared her famous mashed potatoes, her hands deftly mashing the boiled potatoes with butter and cream, then seasoning them just right. There was always a bowl of freshly steamed vegetables green beans, carrots, or peas with a simple yet satisfying sauce made of butter, garlic, and herbs. These sides didn't require fancy ingredients, but the magic was in the way they were cooked, in the way they complemented the flavors of the meal.

In this chapter, I'm sharing some of Grandma's most beloved side dishes the ones that perfectly complemented every Sunday roast, every holiday dinner, and every family gathering. These dishes are not just about taste; they're about comfort, tradition, and the simple joys of sharing a meal with those you love.

Recipes for Comforting Sides:

- **Creamed Spinach Like Grandma Made**
  This creamed spinach recipe was always a hit at Sunday dinner. The spinach was cooked to tender perfection, then combined with a rich, creamy sauce that made it feel like the ultimate comfort food. It was always the perfect accompaniment to the roast meats Grandma made, and the addition of a little garlic and nutmeg gave it an extra layer of flavor.

  Ingredients:
  - 2 pounds fresh spinach, washed and stems removed (or 2 packages frozen spinach)

- 2 tablespoons butter
- 1/4 cup all-purpose flour
- 2 cups heavy cream
- 1/2 teaspoon garlic powder
- 1/4 teaspoon ground nutmeg
- Salt and pepper to taste
- 1/4 cup grated Parmesan cheese

- **Instructions:**
  - If using fresh spinach, blanch it in boiling water for 2-3 minutes, then drain and chop. If using frozen spinach, thaw and drain the spinach well.
  - In a large skillet, melt the butter over medium heat. Stir in the flour and cook for 1-2 minutes until the mixture is golden.
  - Gradually whisk in the heavy cream and bring to a simmer. Cook for 5-7 minutes, until the sauce thickens.

- Add the garlic powder, nutmeg, salt, and pepper. Stir in the spinach and cook for an additional 2-3 minutes, until heated through.

- Stir in the Parmesan cheese and serve hot.

- **Potato Salad: The Picnic Staple**
  Grandma's potato salad was the perfect balance of creamy, tangy, and crunchy. Made with boiled potatoes, mayonnaise, mustard, and a few secret ingredients, this side dish was always the first to disappear at family picnics and barbecues. It was simple but oh-so-satisfying.

  Ingredients:

  - 4 pounds Yukon gold potatoes, peeled and cubed
  - 1/2 cup mayonnaise
  - 1/4 cup Dijon mustard
  - 2 tablespoons apple cider vinegar
  - 1/2 small onion, finely chopped
  - 2 hard-boiled eggs, chopped

- - Salt and pepper to taste
  - 1/4 cup fresh parsley, chopped
- Instructions:
  - Boil the potatoes in salted water for 10-12 minutes, or until fork-tender. Drain and let cool slightly.
  - In a large bowl, mix together the mayonnaise, Dijon mustard, apple cider vinegar, and chopped onion.
  - Add the boiled potatoes, chopped eggs, salt, and pepper to the bowl. Stir gently to combine.
  - Garnish with fresh parsley and refrigerate for at least an hour before serving to allow the flavors to meld.
- Cornbread That Melted in Your Mouth
  Grandma's cornbread was a crowd favorite, always served warm with a pat of butter. It had the perfect crumb soft, moist, and just slightly sweet. It was the perfect accompaniment to any hearty meal, and there was always a little competition over who got the last piece!

Ingredients:

- 1 1/2 cups cornmeal
- 1 cup all-purpose flour
- 1/4 cup sugar
- 1 tablespoon baking powder
- 1/2 teaspoon salt
- 1 cup buttermilk
- 2 large eggs
- 1/4 cup unsalted butter, melted

- Instructions:

  - Preheat the oven to 400°F (200°C). Grease an 8x8-inch baking dish or a cast-iron skillet.
  - In a bowl, combine the cornmeal, flour, sugar, baking powder, and salt.
  - In a separate bowl, whisk together the buttermilk, eggs, and melted butter.

- Pour the wet ingredients into the dry ingredients and stir until just combined.

- Pour the batter into the prepared pan and bake for 20-25 minutes, or until a toothpick inserted into the center comes out clean.

- Let the cornbread cool slightly before slicing and serving.

- **Glazed Carrots with Brown Sugar and Butter**
  These sweet and buttery glazed carrots were always a hit on the dinner table. The brown sugar caramelized as the carrots cooked, giving them a rich, sweet flavor that perfectly balanced the savory dishes.

  Ingredients:

  - 1 pound baby carrots
  - 1/4 cup unsalted butter
  - 1/4 cup brown sugar
  - 1 tablespoon fresh orange juice (optional)
  - Salt and pepper to taste

- **Instructions:**

    - Boil the carrots in salted water for 8-10 minutes, until tender but still crisp.

    - In a large skillet, melt the butter over medium heat. Add the brown sugar and stir to combine.

    - Once the sugar has melted, add the carrots and toss to coat them in the glaze.

    - Add the orange juice, salt, and pepper, and cook for 2-3 minutes, until the glaze thickens slightly.

    - Serve warm.

This chapter showcases the comforting side dishes that made every meal feel complete. These dishes weren't just side items; they were essential parts of the meal that brought everything together. Grandma's kitchen was a place where every dish, no matter how simple, was made with love and care. Let these comforting sides bring warmth and joy to your table, just as they did for our family.

Chapter 7: Preserving the Harvest – Canning and Jams

Grandma's garden was a sanctuary, a place where time seemed to slow down, and the beauty of nature unfolded in rows of ripe tomatoes, plump cucumbers, and fragrant herbs. Every summer, the garden flourished, and the kitchen transformed into a place where the harvest was carefully preserved for the coming months. This was Grandma's way of ensuring that the family would always have fresh produce no matter the season.

Canning and preserving were traditions passed down through generations. While it may seem like a task that requires patience and precision, for Grandma, it was second nature. She knew exactly when the peaches were ripe for canning, when the tomatoes were perfect for making sauce, and when the cucumbers had just the right crunch for pickling. There was no rush in the process, no hurry to get it all done. It was about savoring the moment, honoring the cycle of nature, and sharing the bounty with others.

Every year, as the garden produced its best, Grandma would gather us around to help. We would spend entire afternoons together, washing, peeling, and chopping the fruits and vegetables that would later fill jars and be stored away. The hum of the pressure cooker, the sweet smell of simmering fruits, and the satisfying sound of a jar lid popping sealed in more than just produce it sealed in memories. Those jars, filled with jam, pickles, and sauces, were symbols of Grandma's love and foresight.

In this chapter, I want to share some of Grandma's favorite canning and preserving recipes. These recipes are more than just ways to store food; they are part of a tradition that celebrates the changing seasons and the joy of creating something lasting. Whether you're preserving summer's bounty for the winter months or giving jars of homemade jam as a gift, these recipes will allow you to bring a piece of Grandma's kitchen into your own home.

Recipes for Canning and Jams:

- Homemade Strawberry Jam
    There was nothing like Grandma's strawberry jam, made with fresh, ripe berries picked from her garden. The jam was perfectly sweet with a hint of tartness, and it was thickened just right so it could be spread on toast or served as a

topping for pancakes. The beauty of this jam was that it captured the essence of summer in every jar.

Ingredients:

- 4 cups fresh strawberries, hulled and mashed
- 4 cups granulated sugar
- 1/4 cup lemon juice
- 1 packet pectin (or as per manufacturer's instructions)

- **Instructions:**
  - In a large saucepan, combine the strawberries, sugar, and lemon juice. Bring to a boil, stirring constantly.
  - Once the mixture reaches a rolling boil, add the pectin and continue to cook for another 2-3 minutes, until the jam thickens.
  - Remove from heat and skim off any foam from the top.

- Pour the jam into sterilized jars, leaving about 1/4-inch of space at the top. Seal with lids and process in a boiling water bath for 10 minutes.

- Let the jars cool and store in a cool, dark place for up to a year.

- **Pickled Cucumbers**

  Grandma's pickles were a perfect balance of sweet and tangy, with just the right amount of crunch. These pickles were a staple at family picnics and barbecues, and they were always the first to disappear. Grandma's secret? She used fresh dill from her garden and a touch of garlic to give them extra flavor.

  Ingredients:

  - 8 medium cucumbers, sliced into rounds or spears
  - 2 cups white vinegar
  - 2 cups water
  - 2 tablespoons kosher salt
  - 1 tablespoon sugar

- 3 cloves garlic, smashed
- 2 tablespoons fresh dill, chopped
- 1 teaspoon mustard seeds (optional)
- 1/2 teaspoon crushed red pepper flakes (optional)

- **Instructions:**
  - In a saucepan, combine the vinegar, water, salt, and sugar. Bring to a boil, stirring to dissolve the salt and sugar. Remove from heat and let cool.
  - In sterilized jars, layer the cucumber slices or spears with garlic, dill, mustard seeds, and red pepper flakes (if using).
  - Pour the cooled vinegar mixture over the cucumbers, ensuring they are fully covered.
  - Seal the jars and refrigerate for at least 48 hours before eating. They'll keep for up to 2 weeks in the fridge.

- **Tomato Sauce for Winter**
  Canning tomato sauce was a tradition Grandma never skipped. The smell of ripe tomatoes

simmering on the stove was one of the most comforting things in her kitchen. This sauce, made with fresh garden tomatoes, herbs, and garlic, was perfect for pasta, pizza, or even as a base for soups. It was always a treat to open a jar in the middle of winter and taste a little bit of summer.

Ingredients:

- 10 pounds ripe tomatoes, peeled and chopped
- 1 medium onion, chopped
- 4 garlic cloves, minced
- 1/4 cup olive oil
- 2 teaspoons dried oregano
- 2 teaspoons dried basil
- Salt and pepper to taste
- 2 tablespoons fresh parsley, chopped

- Instructions:
    - Heat olive oil in a large pot over medium heat. Add the onions and garlic, cooking

until softened and fragrant.

- Add the chopped tomatoes, oregano, basil, salt, and pepper. Simmer for 1-2 hours, stirring occasionally, until the sauce thickens and the flavors meld together.

- Once the sauce is ready, use an immersion blender or regular blender to smooth it out if desired.

- Pour the hot sauce into sterilized jars, leaving about 1/2 inch of space at the top. Seal with lids and process in a boiling water bath for 35-40 minutes.

- Let the jars cool and store in a cool, dark place. This sauce will last up to a year when stored properly.

- **Peach Jam**

  When peaches were in season, Grandma would make jars and jars of peach jam. The combination of sweet, ripe peaches with just a hint of vanilla made this jam a family favorite. It was a treat spread on toast in the morning or served as a topping for ice cream in the summer.

  Ingredients:

- 4 cups fresh peaches, peeled and chopped
- 4 cups granulated sugar
- 1/4 cup lemon juice
- 1 teaspoon vanilla extract
- 1 packet pectin

- **Instructions:**

  - In a large pot, combine the peaches, sugar, and lemon juice. Cook over medium heat until the sugar dissolves and the peaches begin to break down.
  - Bring the mixture to a boil and cook for 10-15 minutes until the fruit is soft and the mixture has thickened.
  - Stir in the pectin and vanilla extract, then cook for another 2-3 minutes.
  - Pour the jam into sterilized jars, leaving about 1/4 inch of space at the top. Seal the jars and process in a boiling water bath for 10 minutes.

- Let the jars cool and store in a cool, dark place for up to a year.

This chapter not only highlights the art of canning and preserving but also honors the tradition of taking what nature gives us and turning it into something that can be enjoyed year-round. Each jar, filled with fruits, vegetables, or herbs, holds more than just food; it holds the essence of summer, the labor of love, and the care passed down through generations. Let these recipes help you bring the bounty of each season into your kitchen, just as Grandma did.

Chapter 8: Around the Table – Special Occasions and Holiday Feasts

For Grandma, the kitchen was where memories were made, but the table was where they were shared. Special occasions and holidays were always filled with laughter, storytelling, and, of course, incredible food. Whether it was Christmas, Easter, Thanksgiving, or a simple family gathering, Grandma's table was always set with care, love, and a feast that could rival any restaurant.

Each holiday brought its own unique spread of dishes, but the common thread was always the same: comfort, tradition, and a sense of home. Grandma had a gift for making every occasion feel like a grand celebration. The food wasn't just delicious; it was an expression of love. Every dish, whether it was the creamy mashed potatoes or the decadent pumpkin pie, was made with intention. The love she put into every bite made it clear that these meals were meant to nourish not only the body but also the soul.

I remember Easter Sundays when Grandma would roast a leg of lamb, the garlic and rosemary infusing the air as it slowly cooked. There was always something about the way she set the table, the gleaming china, the crystal glasses, and the family gathered around, ready to eat. Those were the moments that made everything feel right in the world the warmth of family, the comfort of good food, and the joy of being together.

In this chapter, I'm sharing some of the most memorable recipes from Grandma's holiday feasts. These are the dishes that brought the family together year after year, creating traditions that lasted for generations. Whether you're preparing a feast for a special holiday or hosting a family gathering, these recipes will bring the spirit of celebration and togetherness to your table.

Recipes for Special Occasions and Holiday Feasts:

- Grandma's Thanksgiving Stuffing
  This stuffing was the heart of Grandma's Thanksgiving spread. Made with her special blend of bread, herbs, and spices, it was the perfect side to accompany the roast turkey. Every bite was a comforting reminder of the family traditions that made Thanksgiving so special. Grandma's secret was in the perfect balance of flavors — savory, sweet, and just a touch of spice.

Ingredients:

- 1 loaf of day-old bread, cubed
- 1 medium onion, chopped
- 2 celery stalks, chopped
- 1/4 cup unsalted butter
- 2 teaspoons dried sage
- 1 teaspoon dried thyme
- 1/2 teaspoon salt
- 1/4 teaspoon black pepper
- 1/4 teaspoon ground nutmeg
- 1 1/2 cups chicken broth
- 1/2 cup fresh parsley, chopped

- Instructions:

  - Preheat the oven to 350°F (175°C). Grease a 9x13-inch baking dish.

  - In a large skillet, melt the butter over medium heat. Add the onions and celery and cook until softened.

- In a large bowl, combine the cubed bread, herbs, salt, pepper, and nutmeg.

- Add the sautéed onions and celery to the bread mixture, then pour in the chicken broth. Stir until the bread is moistened.

- Pour the stuffing into the prepared baking dish and bake for 30-35 minutes, or until golden brown on top.

- **Christmas Pudding**
Christmas dinner wouldn't have been complete without Grandma's famous Christmas pudding. This rich, spiced dessert, served with brandy butter, was a highlight of every holiday celebration. It was a tradition to make it a few weeks before Christmas, allowing the flavors to deepen and intensify. Grandma always made sure to add a coin to the pudding for luck, a fun tradition that the children loved.

Ingredients:

- 1 cup suet

- 1 cup breadcrumbs

- 1 cup all-purpose flour
- 1 teaspoon ground cinnamon
- 1 teaspoon ground nutmeg
- 1/2 teaspoon salt
- 1/2 cup dark brown sugar
- 1/2 cup raisins
- 1/2 cup currants
- 1/2 cup chopped dried apricots
- 2 large eggs
- 1/2 cup milk
- 1/4 cup brandy
- 1/2 cup treacle or molasses
- 1 coin (wrapped in foil for tradition)

- **Instructions:**
    - In a large bowl, combine all the dry ingredients: suet, breadcrumbs, flour, cinnamon, nutmeg, salt, sugar, raisins,

currants, and apricots.

- Beat the eggs and add them to the dry ingredients, followed by the milk, brandy, and treacle.

- Mix everything together and pour into a greased pudding basin.

- Place the wrapped coin in the mixture, ensuring it's well-covered by the batter.

- Cover the basin with a greased piece of parchment paper and a tight-fitting lid or foil.

- Steam the pudding over simmering water for 6-8 hours, ensuring the water level remains constant.

- Let the pudding cool, then store in a cool, dark place for a few weeks before serving. Reheat by steaming for an additional hour before serving with brandy butter.

- **Easter Lamb with Roasted Vegetables**
  Easter was never complete without Grandma's roast lamb. Tender, juicy, and seasoned with garlic, rosemary, and thyme, the lamb was the centerpiece of our Easter feast. Roasted

alongside it were carrots, parsnips, and potatoes, all glazed in the same aromatic herb mixture, creating a symphony of flavors that perfectly complemented the rich lamb.

Ingredients:

- 1 leg of lamb (5-6 pounds)
- 4 garlic cloves, minced
- 3 tablespoons fresh rosemary, chopped
- 2 tablespoons fresh thyme, chopped
- 1/4 cup olive oil
- 2 teaspoons salt
- 1 teaspoon black pepper
- 6 medium potatoes, peeled and cubed
- 4 carrots, peeled and cut into chunks
- 2 parsnips, peeled and cut into chunks

- Instructions:
    - Preheat the oven to 400°F (200°C).

- In a small bowl, combine the garlic, rosemary, thyme, olive oil, salt, and pepper. Rub this mixture all over the leg of lamb.
- Place the lamb on a roasting pan and surround it with the cubed potatoes, carrots, and parsnips.
- Roast for 1.5-2 hours, or until the lamb reaches your desired doneness (145°F for medium-rare).
- Let the lamb rest for 10-15 minutes before carving. Serve with the roasted vegetables.

- **Baked Ham with Pineapple Glaze**
  This ham was a staple at Grandma's holiday feasts. The sweet pineapple glaze caramelized beautifully on the ham, creating a sticky, flavorful coating that complemented the salty, smoky taste of the meat. Served with mashed potatoes and vegetables, this dish was always the highlight of the meal.

  Ingredients:

    - 1 bone-in ham (8-10 pounds)

- 1 cup brown sugar
- 1/2 cup Dijon mustard
- 1/2 cup pineapple juice
- 1/4 cup apple cider vinegar
- 1/4 teaspoon ground cloves

- **Instructions:**
  - Preheat the oven to 325°F (160°C).
  - Place the ham in a roasting pan and score the surface in a crisscross pattern.
  - In a small saucepan, combine the brown sugar, Dijon mustard, pineapple juice, apple cider vinegar, and cloves. Bring to a simmer and cook for 5-7 minutes, until the glaze thickens.
  - Brush the glaze over the ham and roast for 1.5-2 hours, basting with the glaze every 30 minutes.
  - Let the ham rest for 15 minutes before slicing and serving.

Chapter 9: Simple Pleasures – Everyday Comfort Foods

While holiday feasts and special occasions held a special place in Grandma's heart, it was the everyday meals that truly captured the essence of her cooking. These were the meals that made the house feel like home the comforting, simple dishes that we could count on for breakfast, lunch, or dinner. They were meals for busy weekdays, quiet weekends, and late-night cravings. Yet, no matter how simple the dish, Grandma made each one with the same care and love as if it were a grand celebration.

These dishes were all about familiarity and comfort. Whether it was the classic macaroni and cheese that could feed the whole family or the homemade meatloaf that would warm you up on a chilly evening, these recipes were built on the idea of nourishment — both for the body and the soul. They were meals you could rely on when you needed something quick, something familiar, something that reminded you that you were loved and cared for.

I remember many evenings when Grandma would make a big batch of spaghetti and meatballs. It was a simple meal, but when served with a side of garlic bread and a green salad, it felt like a feast. It was a dish that could be shared, whether it was just the two of us or the entire extended family. For Grandma, it was never about extravagant ingredients; it was about the heart she poured into every meal, the joy of feeding her loved ones, and the warmth of sitting down together at the table.

In this chapter, I'm sharing some of the comforting everyday meals that were staples in Grandma's kitchen. These dishes weren't about showmanship; they were about satisfaction, simplicity, and the joy of sharing a meal with the people you love. These recipes will fill your home with the same warmth and nostalgia that Grandma's kitchen always had, no matter what day of the week it was.

Recipes for Simple Pleasures:

- **Macaroni and Cheese: The Family Favorite**
  Mac and cheese was a family favorite, a dish that could turn any meal into something special. Grandma's version was creamy, cheesy, and perfectly baked with a crunchy golden top. It was comfort food at its finest, perfect for any night when you needed something warm and filling.

  Ingredients:

- 1 pound elbow macaroni
- 3 cups shredded sharp cheddar cheese
- 1 cup grated Parmesan cheese
- 2 cups whole milk
- 1/4 cup butter
- 2 tablespoons all-purpose flour
- 1/2 teaspoon salt
- 1/4 teaspoon black pepper
- 1/2 teaspoon mustard powder
- 1/4 teaspoon paprika
- 1/2 cup breadcrumbs (optional for topping)

- **Instructions:**
  - Preheat the oven to 350°F (175°C). Cook the macaroni according to the package instructions, then drain and set aside.
  - In a large saucepan, melt the butter over medium heat. Add the flour and whisk for

1-2 minutes to form a roux.

- Slowly whisk in the milk, then cook and stir until the mixture thickens, about 5-7 minutes.

- Add the cheddar cheese, Parmesan cheese, salt, pepper, mustard powder, and paprika. Stir until the cheese has melted and the sauce is smooth.

- Combine the cooked macaroni with the cheese sauce, then pour into a greased 9x13-inch baking dish.

- (Optional) Sprinkle the breadcrumbs on top for added crunch, and bake for 25-30 minutes, or until golden and bubbly.

- **Grilled Cheese and Tomato Soup**
A simple, classic meal, this combination was a go-to for cozy nights when we needed a little extra comfort. The creamy tomato soup paired perfectly with the crispy, buttery grilled cheese sandwiches, and it was always made with love and a little extra butter — just the way Grandma made it.

Ingredients for Grilled Cheese:

- 8 slices of white or whole wheat bread
- 4 tablespoons unsalted butter, softened
- 8 slices of cheddar cheese

- **Ingredients for Tomato Soup:**
  - 1 can (28 oz) crushed tomatoes
  - 1 cup chicken broth
  - 1/2 cup heavy cream
  - 1 medium onion, chopped
  - 2 cloves garlic, minced
  - 1 tablespoon olive oil
  - Salt and pepper to taste
  - 1/2 teaspoon dried basil
  - 1/4 teaspoon sugar

- **Instructions for Grilled Cheese:**
  - Butter one side of each slice of bread. Place 2 slices of cheese between two slices of bread, with the buttered sides

facing out.

- Heat a skillet over medium heat. Grill the sandwiches for 3-4 minutes on each side, or until golden brown and the cheese is melted.

- Remove from the skillet and set aside.

- Instructions for Tomato Soup:

    - In a pot, heat the olive oil over medium heat. Add the onions and garlic and sauté until softened, about 5 minutes.

    - Add the crushed tomatoes, chicken broth, basil, sugar, salt, and pepper. Bring to a simmer and cook for 15-20 minutes, allowing the flavors to meld.

    - Stir in the heavy cream, then use an immersion blender to blend the soup until smooth (or leave it chunky if you prefer).

    - Serve the soup hot with the grilled cheese sandwiches.

- Homemade Meatloaf
Grandma's meatloaf was always a crowd-pleaser. It was tender and juicy, made with a blend of beef and pork, and topped with a tangy

ketchup glaze. It was one of those comforting dishes that could easily be reheated for leftovers the next day, and it never failed to make the house smell amazing.

Ingredients:

- 1 pound ground beef
- 1/2 pound ground pork
- 1 cup breadcrumbs
- 1/2 cup milk
- 1/4 cup ketchup
- 1 small onion, finely chopped
- 2 cloves garlic, minced
- 1 egg
- 1 tablespoon Worcestershire sauce
- 1 teaspoon salt
- 1/2 teaspoon black pepper
- 1/4 teaspoon dried thyme

- 1/4 cup ketchup (for topping)

- Instructions:

    - Preheat the oven to 350°F (175°C). In a large bowl, combine the ground beef, ground pork, breadcrumbs, milk, 1/4 cup ketchup, onion, garlic, egg, Worcestershire sauce, salt, pepper, and thyme. Mix well until combined.

    - Shape the mixture into a loaf and place it in a greased 9x5-inch loaf pan.

    - Spread 1/4 cup of ketchup on top of the meatloaf.

    - Bake for 1 hour, or until the meatloaf is cooked through (an internal temperature of 160°F or 71°C).

    - Let the meatloaf rest for 10 minutes before slicing and serving.

- Chicken Pot Pie

  This comforting dish was always a favorite in Grandma's house. The flaky crust, filled with creamy chicken and vegetables, was the perfect meal for a cozy dinner. Grandma's version was made from scratch, with a filling that was rich and hearty, yet perfectly balanced.

Ingredients for Filling:

- 2 cups cooked chicken, shredded
- 1 cup frozen peas
- 1 cup frozen carrots
- 1/2 cup celery, chopped
- 1 small onion, chopped
- 1/4 cup unsalted butter
- 1/4 cup all-purpose flour
- 2 cups chicken broth
- 1/2 cup milk
- 1/2 teaspoon salt
- 1/4 teaspoon black pepper
- 1/4 teaspoon dried thyme

- **Ingredients for Crust:**
  - 1 1/2 cups all-purpose flour

- 1/2 teaspoon salt
- 1/2 cup unsalted butter, cold and cubed
- 3-4 tablespoons ice water

- **Instructions for Filling:**
  - In a skillet, melt the butter over medium heat. Add the onion, celery, peas, and carrots. Cook for 5-7 minutes until softened.
  - Stir in the flour and cook for 1-2 minutes, until golden.
  - Gradually whisk in the chicken broth and milk, and cook for another 5 minutes, until the mixture thickens.
  - Stir in the shredded chicken, salt, pepper, and thyme. Remove from heat and set aside.

- **Instructions for Crust:**
  - In a bowl, combine the flour and salt. Cut in the butter until the mixture resembles coarse crumbs.

- Gradually add the ice water, a tablespoon at a time, until the dough comes together.
- Roll out the dough on a floured surface to fit a 9-inch pie dish.
- Pour the chicken filling into the pie dish and top with the dough. Trim and crimp the edges to seal.
- Cut a few slits in the top to allow steam to escape.
- Bake at 375°F (190°C) for 30-35 minutes, or until the crust is golden brown.

This chapter celebrates the comforting simplicity of everyday meals dishes that are hearty, filling, and always made with love. These recipes may be simple, but they are full of the love and care that Grandma always put into every meal. Whether it's the mac and cheese that became a family tradition or the homemade meatloaf that turned any evening into a special occasion, these dishes are timeless favorites that will bring warmth to your table.

Chapter 10: The Passing of a Legacy – Keeping Grandma's Spirit Alive

As time goes on, those we love most are not always with us physically. But the essence of who they were their kindness, their warmth, and their wisdom can live on, carried forward by the recipes, stories, and traditions they've passed down. Grandma's kitchen was her domain, but it was also a place where memories were made, and those memories are what keep her spirit alive.

When Grandma could no longer stand in the kitchen, we were the ones who took over. We didn't just follow her recipes we embraced them. Each time we made one of her famous dishes, we remembered the sound of her voice, the way she measured ingredients with her heart, and the love she poured into every meal. The recipes weren't just instructions they were part of her legacy.

I think about how much of who I am today was shaped by the time spent with Grandma in that kitchen. The lessons she taught weren't just about cooking; they were about patience, about taking pride in your work, about creating something from nothing, and about the power of nurturing others through food. She taught us that a meal shared with family was the greatest gift you could give. Every dish was a reflection of her love, and every meal was an opportunity to show how much we cared.

As we gather to cook and share meals today, we are reminded that Grandma's spirit lives on in each of us. She lives on in the recipes she passed down, in the love we put into our own cooking, and in the joy we find in gathering around the table. These recipes are more than just food; they are a bridge between the past and the future, a way to honor the legacy of a woman who gave so much of herself to others.

In this chapter, I'll reflect on the most important lessons Grandma taught us and how we can continue to carry her legacy forward. Cooking her recipes is one way to honor her, but it's also about continuing her traditions, making our own memories, and passing down what we've learned to the next generation.

Lessons from Grandma's Kitchen:

- **The Importance of Patience**
  One of the greatest lessons I learned from Grandma was the importance of patience. Whether it was waiting for bread to rise or letting a pot of soup simmer for hours, Grandma understood that good things take time. She taught us that cooking was never a race; it was about being present, allowing flavors to develop,

and savoring the process, not just the end result. In our fast-paced world, that lesson is more important than ever. Cooking is about slowing down, enjoying the moment, and appreciating the process of creating something beautiful.

- **The Power of Love in Cooking**
  Every dish Grandma made was infused with love. She didn't just cook to feed us; she cooked to nurture us. Food was her way of saying, "I care about you." Whether it was a pot of soup when we were sick or a homemade cake for our birthday, Grandma used food as a way to show her love. The act of cooking became a form of communication, a way to express emotions and offer comfort. Today, when we cook, we do so with that same intention — to nurture, to care, and to connect with those we love.

- **The Tradition of Sharing Meals Together**
  Grandma always believed in the power of family meals. She understood that sitting down to a meal together wasn't just about eating; it was about connecting, about sharing stories, about laughing, and about being present with one another. Those Sunday dinners, those holiday feasts, those casual weeknight meals — they were all about bringing us together. In a world that often pulls us in different directions, Grandma's kitchen was a place where we could all come together, put aside our busy lives, and

simply enjoy each other's company. The tradition of sharing meals is something we continue to honor in our own homes.

- **The Art of Cooking with What You Have**
  Grandma was never one to waste anything. She knew how to make a meal out of whatever was available, turning even the simplest ingredients into something special. She taught us to be resourceful in the kitchen, to make do with what we had, and to find joy in the simplicity of food. This lesson wasn't just about frugality; it was about appreciating what you had, being grateful for it, and making the most of it. Cooking with what you have can bring creativity into the kitchen and allow you to experiment and make something wonderful with the ingredients you have on hand.

- **The Joy of Teaching Others**
  Grandma was always eager to teach us how to cook. She believed that cooking was something that should be shared, that everyone should have the chance to experience the joy of making a meal from scratch. Whether it was teaching us how to bake a pie or showing us how to knead dough, Grandma was patient and kind in sharing her knowledge. This is a lesson we carry with us — the importance of passing on what we know, whether it's a recipe, a skill, or a tradition. Cooking together not only builds connections but

also creates opportunities to pass down knowledge to the next generation.

Carrying Grandma's Legacy Forward:

- **Passing Down Recipes**
  The most direct way to honor Grandma's legacy is by continuing to make her recipes. Each time we bake her famous chocolate chip cookies or cook her comforting chicken soup, we are keeping her memory alive. We're not just following her instructions; we're embracing the love and care she poured into every dish. Each time we share her food with others, we're sharing a piece of her heart.

- **Creating New Traditions**
  While we honor Grandma's recipes, it's also important to create our own traditions. As we gather around the table with our families, we can add new dishes to the table and continue to build memories. Whether it's hosting a family potluck or making a new recipe each holiday season, we continue to keep the spirit of family meals alive.

- **Cooking with Love**
  The most important lesson Grandma taught us was that cooking is an act of love. We don't need

to be professional chefs to create memorable meals; all we need is love. Every time we cook, we can channel that love into the meal, making it special for those we serve. Cooking is about connecting with others, about showing care, and about creating moments of joy that will last long after the meal is over.

As you turn the pages of this book and recreate Grandma's recipes in your own kitchen, I hope you feel her spirit with you. Let her legacy live on in the meals you cook, in the traditions you create, and in the love you share with others. Grandma may no longer be with us physically, but her spirit will always be present in the meals we make, the lessons we teach, and the memories we carry forward.

Chapter 11: Conclusion – A Legacy of Flavor, Love, and Memories

As we come to the end of this journey through Grandma's kitchen, it's impossible not to reflect on everything that we've learned not just about recipes, but about life, love, and tradition. Each dish we've shared, each memory we've revisited, is a testament to the lasting impact that food and family can have on our lives.

Grandma's kitchen was never just about cooking; it was about creating a space where memories were made, lessons were learned, and love was shared. Her recipes were her way of passing down a piece of herself a way to ensure that the spirit of family, togetherness, and love would continue long after the dishes were cleared and the table was empty.

As we recreate these meals in our own kitchens, we carry with us not only the flavors of the past but the wisdom of Grandma's approach to life: to cook with love, to share with others, and to always appreciate the simple joys that come from being together. Her legacy lives on in every recipe we pass down, in every family meal we share, and in every moment we spend around the table.

The act of cooking is an act of love, and through these pages, we've learned that the ingredients we use are just as important as the memories we create. Each meal is an opportunity to connect with those we love, to reflect on our shared history, and to honor the generations that came before us. And as we continue to pass these recipes down, we not only keep Grandma's spirit alive, but we create new traditions and memories that will be carried forward into the future.

It is with this spirit of love and legacy that I leave you with the hope that you will continue to cook with heart, just as Grandma did. That you will cherish the moments spent in the kitchen, teaching others, and sharing meals with those who matter most. That you will embrace the lessons passed down through generations and create a legacy of your own, one filled with flavor, love, and memories that will last forever.

Final Thoughts:

Food is a universal language it speaks to the soul, connects us to our past, and provides a sense of comfort and belonging. Through these recipes, we've not only learned how to create delicious dishes but how to appreciate the simple joys of life, how to honor tradition, and how to show love through the act of cooking.

Grandma's kitchen was a space of love, laughter, and learning. And now, as you embark on your own journey in the kitchen, you carry her legacy with you. Whether you're preparing a Sunday dinner, baking a pie, or making jam, remember that every meal you create has the potential to bring joy, build connections, and create memories. So, cook with love, share with those you care about, and keep the legacy of Grandma's kitchen alive in your own home.

Thank you for joining me on this journey through *Grandma's Kitchen Chronicles*. May your own kitchen be filled with the same warmth, love, and delicious flavors that Grandma's was. Here's to many more meals, memories, and moments of love shared around the table.

Printed in Dunstable, United Kingdom